living
community

living
community

thirty think pieces for moving
from dreams to reality

joseph schaeffer, ph.d.

foreword by paul born

BPS
books
Toronto & New York
www.bpsbooks.com

Published in 2014 by BPS Books
Toronto and New York
www.bpsbooks.com
A division of Bastian Publishing Services Ltd.

ISBN 978-1-927483-85-5

Cataloguing-in-Publication Data available from Library and Archives Canada.

Cover: Daniel Crack, Kinetics Design

Text design and typesetting: PressBooks

Cover illustration: Wikipediacommons, Mauro Cateb

Printed in Canada

For
Eric, Ani, and Tes

contents

part two: creative communication

part three: end notes

foreword

by paul born

Living community is not easy to do or create. To live in community, one must have the desire to be part of a community, to engage in the lives of others on an ongoing basis, to care and to be cared for. It is an act of recognizing that the needs of the many are as important as the needs of one and of entering into a relationship with others over time who feel the same. In turn, a living community is one that is active, constant, and vibrant. It requires time to both live in community and benefit from being together.

Many of us dream about community: either the communities we were once a part of or the communities we would like to be a part of. The reality today is that most of us live lives of isolation and have replaced deep community with shallow community. We visit our families far too seldom because we live so far away from them or are just too busy. Our friends, even our best friends, fill their time with the many activities available to us, moving from one activity to the other or cocooning in front of the television or computer. Neighbours often are only people who live beside us, and we often tread softly in order not to bother one another.

Realizing the dream of living community is possible. When we engage in the lives of people we care about on an ongoing basis and come to know their story deeply, we evoke, in ourselves and in others, the desire for ongoing connection ... we take the time to be a part of one another's unfolding story. To be a part of someone's unfolding story is to enjoy them, to have fun together. It is to care for them when they are in need and to reach out to them when we are in need. It is to open ourselves to their story and them to ours.

We need community; it makes us healthier, happier, and even more secure economically. The future survival of our planet will depend on a living community. We cannot solve the environmental and economic issues facing us alone. When we love people who are in our community, our desire is to reach out together to build the kind of places where life thrives. This is the living community that will ultimately save our planet. We must make the dream of community a reality.

Joe Schaeffer understands, more than anyone else I know, the essence of community and the qualities of character of living community. He has travelled the world engaging with more than fifteen thousand people, has interviewed Nobel laureates, and has thought deeply about how the people of this world might live together in harmony. As Joe writes in this book, "We need community if we are to alleviate the ocean of pain and suffering around the world ... We need community if we are to prepare a better world for our children, a world that is just and joyful."

Joe has spent the better part of his life teaching the qualities of character and creative communication to help people understand community as a way of living that "we carry with us all the time." I am a student of Joe's. I first met him when I was reading the manuscript of his first book, *The Stone People: Living Together in a Different World*. I was so taken by his ideas that I started attending his daylong seminars and then a special five-day Train-the-Trainer workshop to learn how I might incorporate his ideas and approach into my own teaching. In midlife, I went back to school to complete a Master's degree and chose Royal Roads University largely because Joe was teaching there at the time. Joe became my thesis advisor and helped me write what was to become my first book, *Leaderful Communities*. It was this thesis that shaped the thinking that would eventually inspire the founding of Tamarack—An Institute for Community Engagement. Joe has influenced much of my work and shepherded many of the ideas we hold dear at Tamarack.

For all of those interested in community, this book is for you.

If you want to understand the qualities of character that Joe explores, and in turn to "carry community with you all the time," read this book.

If you are a community developer and want to understand how to make community useful in creating better cities, restoring our environment, or making our neighbourhoods safer, this book is for you.

If you head a charity or faith community or are a business owner shepherding a team, the ideas expressed in this book will make you a much better leader.

The world needs this book. On behalf of Tamarack, I am pleased to say that we are honoured to be part of the team that is bringing it to you.

Much joy,
Paul Born

Paul Born is President of Tamarack—An Institute for Community Engagement, and author of the newly released *Deepening Community: Finding Joy Together in Chaotic Times.*

introduction

I read the Pooh Bear books to my children when they were young.

Pooh Bear, Tigger, and their friends lived together in a small community—each distinct and unique—tied together in friendship by their common humanity.

Pooh liked to go on "explores," especially when the smell of honey was in the air. Maybe knowledge is honey to me. Or understanding the human condition. Either way, I have been on an explore since I was a very young boy.

I remember asking my mother, when I was about four, "Why do people fight so much?"

The question tumbled around inside as I grew older. By the time I was a teenager it had taken a positive turn: "How can we get along better with each other?"

In my early twenties, with the benefits of higher education, my explore became more sophisticated: "How can we be more co-operative and creative with each other? How can we enjoy competition without animosity? How can we work through our differences, our conflicts, together? How can we make decisions that serve us well?"

Then, some years ago, when I was about forty, as a result of working with poor people and the disenfranchised, I realized these questions had become very personal to me: "How can I be truly humane within and with others, everywhere, all the time?"

Nowadays, because I am committed to social, economic, and political justice, I ask the larger question as well: "How can human beings be truly humane within and with each other everywhere, all the time?" That's the heart of the matter for me on this, my biggest explore. In some ways it has been there all along.

I have come to believe to be truly human and truly humane, we must learn to live in a special kind of community like Pooh Bear, Tigger, and the others. We have to create fundamental values together and live those values with each other every day. And we have to sustain them with creative communication no matter what challenges we face in this complex world.

I haven't been alone all these years, of course. My thinking has been influenced by literally thousands of people, from family and friends to students, teachers, and colleagues to participants in workshops and educational programs and to scholars, artists, musicians, writers, scientists, diplomats, and business people—people I admire from many facets of life and many places in the world. Learning with them has been part of the journey.

Living Community is a collection of Think Pieces inspired by conversations with these people. It emphasizes community as a way of living we carry with us all the time rather than community as a thing connected to economy, ideology, shared values, or geography.

I begin workshops with a simple question: "What would people be like within and with each other in a world you would like to be part of?" I have asked this question of people from many ethnic groups and cultures, of Muslims and Christians, of business people and blue-collar workers, of prisoners and police, of pretty much every kind of person you can imagine from every walk of life. They all mention the same fundamental ways of living, which, over the years, I have summarized as five qualities of character that seem to be at the very heart of living community. These are the focus of the first part of this book.

Genuine interest emphasizes self-understanding and deep interest in understanding others.

Acknowledgement highlights the critical importance of seeing and knowing diverse points of view without accepting all of them as right.

Deep empathy makes it possible for us to become as others, to see through their eyes in the deepest sense possible.

Altruism is a powerful quality of character that allows us to achieve self-actualization and to support others as they do so, too.

And *mutual trust* brings together trust of others and trust of self in the presence of others.

A sense of oneness is the "tie that binds" these qualities together. And together they make it possible for us to "live community" wherever we are. These qualities seem to flourish when we engage in creative communication, the subject of the second part of the book. Creative communication is

based on a theory of communication that emphasizes mutual creation and discovery of meaning no
matter what the subject of discourse. I describe
this theory in three Think Pieces. Then I explore
two key implications of the theory. The first is that
we can converse as partners without attempting to
have power over each other. The second is that we
can celebrate our equality as human beings without losing the treasure of diversity. Openness to
novelty rather than safety in prediction is automatic in this approach. Unique experience and
shared meaning live side by side.

Decision-making is transformed through the
exploration and use of creative communication.
The last four Think Pieces in the second part
include brief descriptions of twelve ways people
can explore differences and find solutions they
feel good about together.

Three End Notes, in the third part, explore
assumptions about the sources of and the nature
of meaning in creative communication.

Living Community is avowedly idealistic, even
utopian. But it needs to be written. We need community if we are to alleviate the ocean of pain and
suffering around the world. We need community
if we are to come to our senses and work together

to create solutions to the myriad issues and problems facing us today. We need community if we
are to prepare a better world for our children, a
world that is just and joyful.

part one:
living community

communities and community

*The real voyage of discovery consists not of seek-
ing new landscapes but in having new eyes.*
—Marcel Proust

Most of us think of communities as things
made up of people who come together for various
reasons—for example, biological and social kin-
ship, the desire to live in a particular location, economic necessity, shared values and beliefs, and so
forth. These are the reasons Pooh Bear, Tigger,
and their friends live together. And it's wonderful.
But this kind of natural community doesn't always
happen. We no longer grow up next door to peo-

ple who remain our neighbours from birth. We no longer marry our high school sweethearts. We move from place to place and change employment several times during our lives. And sometimes we don't have time to build a community with others.

So let me suggest another kind of community that can happen anywhere, anytime, with anyone. Let's call it "living community."* Living community is not tied to place, time, or circumstance. It does not depend on definitions of categories like gender, age, ethnicity, or culture. When people live community they are responsible as individuals and respectful of others as a matter of course. They carry community within wherever they go. When they meet others who do the same they feel community instantly.

What are the values these people celebrate? How do they wish to live together? At the beginning of my explore of community and communication I ask a simple question:

What would people be like within and with each other if they "lived community" this way—in families, schools, places of work, neighbourhoods, gatherings of any kind?

*Thanks to my friend Paul Born for this expression.

As I mentioned in the introduction, I've asked this question of more than fifteen thousand people over the past twenty years or so, women and men of all ages from many parts of the world, people with dark and light skin, wealthy entrepreneurs and unemployed people living in the streets, Aboriginal people and recent settlers in new lands, police officers and convicted felons, single parents and couples in their seventies with grandchildren—in one case, fifty-four of them. Most people give the same answers: "I would like people to be interesting and clear. I want them to be good listeners and accepting of differences. They should be open, honest, empathetic, and compassionate. They must be kind and loving, trusting and worthy of trust. They should be serious about life but at the same time be able to have fun." Most of us would rather not live with people who are controlling, judgemental, prejudiced, and vengeful. We have to sometimes, but we would rather not.

How can we be the way we want to be?

genuine interest: i bet to i wonder

"Hello" is a new beginning, a path to discovery.
—Jean Houston

My partner shared a saying with me several years ago. It went something like this: "I don't want to know how much money you make. I want to know what makes your heart sing."

This seems like a good first step to living community. Get beneath the values associated with the material world that so often permeate social small talk. Speak and listen, instead, to the heart and soul.

I call this experience *genuine interest*—a fundamental quality of character in living community.

We so easily give in to the pattern, the stereotypical opening, the usual agenda. "Hello," I say to you. And the me who likes to stay ahead of the game is already drawing conclusions. "What a warm-hearted person she seems to be. I wonder if she works at the university. Probably not; she doesn't look like an intellectual." Or, to be negative, "Her hair looks silly. She must be a floozy. Probably not too bright."

The social science grapevine says human beings speak over eighty-five thousand words to themselves each day. Seventy per cent of these words are about other people. Sixty to seventy per cent of these words about other people are negative. Essentially, if the grapevine is to be believed, we spend much of each day finding fault with those around us in the privacy of self-talk.

Genuine interest is an opening into a completely new way of connecting with others. "Hello," I say to you. And deep inside, I am open to a world I could never predict. I wonder who you are. I wonder what your life is like. This doesn't mean I come up to you and stare into your eyes and ask, "What strikes awe into you?" Rather, I carry genuine interest within me as I say hello. And you can see it in my eyes.

When I do this you sense the spaciousness in me. We are just two people coming together for a moment in time.

Sounds so simple, doesn't it? But the implications can be profound. As I listen to your words I begin to create a sense of you. The more I see and listen, the more fascinated I become. My negative self-talk disappears. My genuine interest in you is unending.

- *What is the most important thing you learned from your parents or those who cared for you when you were young?*
- *What do you think we should be doing with our children so they become good ancestors?*
- *How long has your longest friendship lasted? Why has it lasted so long?*
- *What do you value most about the work you do?*
- *What do you find intolerable?*
- *What do you fear?*
- *What do these words mean to you: duty, power, spirit, love?*

And on … Tell me more. After all, you are a human being. My explore with you could go on forever.

A child's activity comes to mind when I think of genuine interest. It is called the ABCs. It goes like this. We sit in a circle. The object of the game is to get as far as we can in the alphabet. Any person can say any letter, but the letters have to be said sequentially.

Participants immediately come up with ways to organize the process: "We take turns in order around the circle. We raise our hands if we want to speak." And so on. So we try. And we get through the alphabet, but we don't have any fun.

So we try once more, with three simple rules this time. Anybody can say any letter at random, and, again, they must be said sequentially. And if any two or more say a letter together (at the same time), we have to go back to the beginning.

We try a few times without success. Then, in concert, we realize that to succeed we have to practice the deepest listening possible—with our minds, hearts, bodies, and souls. We use the meanings in the Chinese character for "to listen" as our guide.*

*The Chinese character for "to listen" consists of five sub-characters with the meanings "you, eyes, ears, undivided attention, heart."

The circle becomes silent. The atmosphere is beautifully relaxed and intense at the same time. Slowly we begin to say letters, and because we are listening deeply now, we get through the alphabet completely more often than not. And we are ecstatic.

In *Island*, Aldous Huxley wrote of a character who trained his parrot to say "Pay attention" every so often. That's what we all have to do if we wish to live community. We have to pay attention more deeply than we imagined possible.

3

genuine interest:
beginnings

Life is a faint tracing on the surface of mystery.
—Annie Dillard

I had an interesting experience recently that demonstrates the wonder of genuine interest. I was seated next to a young mother with her infant on a four-hour flight to the West Coast. About an hour after we took off, the baby began to fuss and cry. Several folks nearby, busy working on their laptops, sighed loudly and shuffled in their seats, as if to say, "Will you please do something to control your child?" I held my watch in front of the baby. She took it immediately and, of course, put it in her mouth. She studied and played with the watch for almost ten minutes.

"What happened?" I asked myself. "When I was a child I found a watch fascinating for ten minutes. Now that I'm an adult I look at your face for a second and move on. Even another human being is unworthy of my interest for very long."

At birth, all of us are dependent on the protection and nurturance of a caring adult. That place of total safety and well-being is the foundation of our curiosity about the world. Babies at certain stages seem to be curious about everything. Most parents are familiar with this desire for exploration.

Tragically, some infants and young children are abandoned emotionally or abused by those entrusted to care for them. But even those born into good and loving families can become lured into the parts of culture that emphasize indoctrination rather than creativity and the celebration of human potential. Over time the innate and fundamental capacity for genuine interest recedes and becomes dormant. We do not have the time or curiosity to wonder or explore any more.

Years ago, I was teaching in a small liberal arts college in Vermont. As part of our commitment to youth at the time, my partner and I organized the Vermont Governor's Institute on International Affairs for high school students from throughout the state. On the recommendation of a number of respected colleagues, we invited Tarzie Vittachi, a well-known journalist and writer from Sri Lanka, to be the keynote speaker. At the time, Tarzie was the Assistant Deputy Director of UNICEF. He turned out to be a wonderful speaker and a wonderful man—clear and wise.

Tarzie joined us in our home for a quiet dinner at the end of the day. At one point he paused a moment and said, "Joseph, you seem so tired."

"I am a bit burned out," I admitted. "I've been teaching in a very intensive setting for almost fifteen years."

"If you could do anything you wanted for the next year or so," he asked, "what would you do?"

I told him about a project I had been working on for twenty years. Every time I saw a great painting, heard a wonderful concert, read an interesting novel, noticed a great scientist, became aware of a successful and humane person in business or government, I wrote questions. I hoped to explore these questions with the people who created the paintings, performed the concerts, wrote the novels, indeed, with all the people I'd come to admire in my life.

"Do this," he said. "Do it now."

So I took a year's sabbatical, and off I went on a wonderful explore.

I contacted fifty-six individuals, hoping a handful might grant me a few hours of their time. Imagine my surprise when nearly everyone said, "Come ahead." The outcomes were beyond anything I could have imagined.

Ilya Prigogine, winner of a Nobel Prize for his theory of dissipative structures, spoke about his fascination with pre-Columbian art. Madeleine L'Engle, whose ideas about writing have received critical acclaim, spoke movingly and insightfully about her grandchildren. I had intended to explore the history of general systems theory with Ervin László. When I learned he had been a concert pianist, I could not wait to hear about the meaning of music in his life.

For me, genuine interest led to a pathway beyond the world of personality and accomplishment—fascinating and important as this is—into a more expansive realm of creativity and possibility. I felt like that little boy again going on a Pooh Bear explore, consumed by wonder and a deep interest in the world.

4

acknowledgement: i judge to i learn

The good life is one inspired by love and guided by knowledge.
—Bertrand Russell

Acknowledgement is a second important quality of character in living community.

I have chosen the word "acknowledgement" rather than "acceptance" or "tolerance" for good reason. We all must agree to abide by certain rules and patterns of behaviour in any society. It doesn't matter who we are, where we come from, what our gender or ethnicity, what our politics, what our level of wealth—we simply are required to do certain things and not permitted to do others in some places at some times.

And in any society we must recognize the differences in values, beliefs, and actions that make a difference and the differences that don't make a difference. In any society we can acknowledge values, beliefs, and actions without accepting all of them as right.

Let's explore a tough issue to bring acknowledgement to life. In some societies newly married couples killed any female baby born to them until they had a male child, a practice biologists and social scientists call female infanticide. When I first came across this custom, my reaction was one of visceral aversion. I could not begin to accept it.

When people do not live community in a society, they claim the right to translate such "natural" visceral aversion into a universal moral principle. "That's just wrong, period," they say. They do not try to understand the custom.

When people live community, they acknowledge and try to understand the practice in a cultural setting in which it was present for thousands of years to keep a population in check—to keep it within the carrying capacity of the environment. Obviously, female infanticide leads to fewer adult females to have babies. That's why it was accepted as right by some people. But it does not need to be accepted as right today.

Indeed, with three thousand years of Oriental philosophy and two thousand years of Western philosophy behind us, and with the teachings of those who have experienced deep layers of consciousness available to us, we may well determine no society should continue to practice female infanticide under any circumstances. But we come to this conclusion as responsible human beings. We continue to acknowledge the beliefs and values of those who have lived differently from us for thousands of years. We can make the distinction between acknowledgement and understanding, on the one hand, and total acceptance of every belief, value, and behaviour, on the other.

Let's continue our exploration with an imaginary journey. People from many cultures and traditions are standing on the edge of an empty space. We may call this space Canada or the United States or Argentina or India at some point, but at the moment it has no name at all. No one has ever lived in this space.

On a signal from some outside source, everyone steps into the empty space and walks around together, in silence at first. Then, carefully, they begin to converse.

Together they ask a fundamental question: "How shall we live community with each other?" We are different from each other as individuals but equal as human beings. We are interested in each other. We acknowledge and try to understand each other. We cannot know for sure what will happen next. Still, we must experience and create values, customs, and laws together that work for all of us.

I have been told by some this "naïve" exercise is of no practical use. The trends of our times are not mere fabrications. Some people were here first. Others, with new ways, came later. Everyone has used illegitimate power to gain and solidify control in the past, and they will continue to do so.

Of course they are right in the "real world." But each of us has a choice as to what values we embrace in our lives. We all have small pockets of influence — in our families, our schools, our places of work. We can choose to live differently, if only for moments in time. "Whose real world?" I want to ask. Maybe I can live community with some people some of the time.

acknowledgement in "real life"

There are very few times when the higher good of yours and the higher good of mine are in conflict.
—Eleanor Hamilton

One of the most powerful experiences I have had in the workshops I do centred on acknowledgement.

Sikh and non-Sikh legionnaires near Vancouver, British Columbia, had been in serious conflict. The non-Sikhs had refused to let the Sikhs enter the Legion with their turbans on. They said it was disrespectful to those who had died in war.

There was great commotion about this in the community, fanned by the press.

I was asked by a friend in the BC Ministry of Attorney General's office if I would do conflict resolution with the key people on each side, fifteen Sikhs and fifteen non-Sikhs. I said, "No, but I will facilitate a workshop focused on community and creative communication." The Ministry agreed and off we went.

During the first five days we did a variety of experiential activities on genuine interest, acknowledgement, and deep empathy. We also learned creative communication. We talked together as persons, acknowledging differences in values and beliefs. We listened deeply in story circles.

We began the sixth day with an activity in which the group divides into pairs. Then each person in the pairs talks about their hopes and dreams. After each person speaks, the other person acknowledges their hopes and dreams and wishes them well. This is a simple but extremely powerful activity. It is deeply moving to have someone truly acknowledge your hopes and dreams without negative judgement. I have seen many tears of joy as people do this.

I felt apologetic about this at the time, but I manipulated the participants a bit when they were choosing partners for this activity. I asked the non-Sikh man who had stood in the door of the Legion to refuse entry to Sikhs and the man who had stood opposite him at the door to pair off.

When these two men met each other on the first day of the workshop, the non-Sikh spoke firmly to the Sikh. "I have no problem with your coming to this country," he said, "but if you want to live here you should learn our customs and abide by them."

And the Sikh man replied just as firmly, "We were good enough to fight and die beside you in the Second World War with our turbans on."

And so the lines were drawn.

Now here they were, the two combatants, face to face. The Sikh man, an elderly retired colonel who had just lost his wife and was becoming a bit frail with time, told his hopes and dreams to the non-Sikh man. The non-Sikh man, a young, ruddy-faced Irishman, told his hopes and dreams to the Sikh.

When the young man finished, the old Sikh said, with genuine sincerity, "I hope you get what you want in life."

The young man looked at the Sikh for a moment, and then, with a quiet voice and in absolute sincerity replied, "Right back at ya, man."

At the end of the workshop, we set aside twenty minutes to talk about the turban issue. There was no wrangling, no jockeying for position, no conflict resolution. Rather, thirty human beings engaged in creative communication and, in the process, searched for, discovered, and explored new meaning together. Their disagreements had long since disappeared.

The next year, incidentally, the participants walked hand in hand in the Remembrance Day parade.

6

deep empathy in
community

*A student said to his Rabbi, "I love you so much,
Rabbi."*

*The Rabbi responded, "My son, do you know
what hurts me?"*

*And the student said, "Rabbi, all I want to
do is tell you how much I love you and you con-
fuse me with irrelevant questions about hurt."*

*"My question was neither confusing nor
irrelevant," the Rabbi explained. "For if you do
not know what hurts me, how can you love me?"*
—Madeleine L'Engle

I have had the honour of sitting in hundreds
of story circles. During a circle, we pass a symbolic
stone from person to person. When she is holding

the stone, a person may say anything she wishes to say. It is her time. All others will be present, bearing witness as they sense the world from within her eyes.

Over and over I have heard people speak from such a deep place within, seeming to tap the very essence of their lives. I have come to understand the power of *deep empathy*, the third quality of character in creating an environment that is safe from reprisal and, perhaps even more importantly, safe from the judgement of others.

I wonder if deep empathy is present at birth. Parents speak of the profound connection they feel with newborn babies. When they hold a newborn and feel joy, the newborn often registers a soft and palpable openness. The same thing happens with other emotions. When a parent feels upset or confused, for example, the newborn often fusses or cries.

Deep empathy is certainly a potential in human beings, perhaps as a product of Ernst Mayr's "open pre-programming." He used the phrase to refer to a potential for some attribute not necessarily present at birth to become available during the life of an individual.

Most people are wary of being open and honest in our contemporary society. It can seem frighteningly risky to be vulnerable in a world based on illegitimate power and domination. One who shows feelings too openly is considered to be weak, immature, or, at the very least, inappropriate.

All of which begs the question: How can people expect to be truly co-operative and creative with each other if they cannot and will not be open and honest with each other? And how can they be open and honest with each other if they are afraid to be vulnerable? "If I let you know who I am, you might take advantage of me." That's the culture we live in.

I imagine a world in which we can be vulnerable and clear. But that world is elusive today. An example: Suppose I have applied for a new position as manager in my company. After I do so, another person comes along and applies for the same job. Now, I know that person would do the job better than me. So I go to the CEO and I tell him how qualified the other person is and suggest that I stand down. In the real world I could never do this. I would jeopardize my own position by appearing to lack confidence and commitment. Honesty is by no means the best policy all the time.

7

foundations of
deep empathy

*When I feel your empathy, something is released
in me. You dignify me. You permit me to emerge.*
—Karl Eric Knutsson

When people live community, they recognize,
acknowledge, and allow the full complexity and
depth of human emotional experience. They do
not feel embarrassed when someone has the
courage to show an emotion. And they certainly
do not pity or judge her.

Still, it is not always easy to keep the heart
open and accepting and, at the same time, keep
from getting hooked on the drama of someone's

story. But deep empathy is not sympathy or even compassion. And it is not Emotional Intelligence. An individual feels neither for nor with another. She strives for something deeper. She strives to become "as" the other in her very being.

It is as if we sit side by side with each other rather than face to face. We are present; we bear witness as someone tells her story, gets something off her chest, or, at times, heals herself of pain and suffering from the past.

I was sitting next to a teenage girl recently in a community circle. As I listened to her story of abuse at the hands of an older man, I became concerned. She was leaning forward, as if her body hurt, crying through the words she spoke. I broke my empathy and knelt in front of her.

"Are you OK?" I asked.

"I'm not finished yet," was her reply—irritated.

Later, I again became concerned and knelt in front of her a second time. "Are you OK?" I asked again.

"I'm ready to come home," she said. A broad smile replaced her tears as she settled back in her chair. She knew who she was. She knew what she needed to do.

I could have trusted the power of deep empathy all along. I could have sat quietly beside her and allowed the unfolding of her experience while she healed herself.

Sometimes a person's experience is so intense and potentially self-destructive that she needs to find professional help in the form of therapy or medication. But when a person knows she can care for herself, when she needs a healing circle rather than a therapist's couch, the simple empathic presence of others as witnesses can provide the safety and support she needs.

I wonder how many appointments with health-care professionals and how much the use of medications might be avoided if we could simply treat each other with genuine interest, acknowledgement, and deep empathy all the time.

8

stories of deep empathy

Story work is quiet work.
It is something we do together,
to share essential meanings in our lives.
—Ralph John, First Nations Elder

I have come to believe that deep empathy is a critical pathway to our common humanity. Again and again I have observed people in workshops move from polarized positions of stereotyping and racism to mutual regard and appreciation, even open affection.

I remember a police officer, for example, who had been asked to attend a workshop I facilitated with officers from a community-policing branch along with members of the non-police public. When he came into the room, he took me aside to let me know he already knew what he needed to know about "multiculturalism." He'd been to workshops like this before, he explained, and they were "a bunch of bull." He was there only because he had to be.

To his credit, he did participate in the activities in the workshop. By the time we got to the story circle, he was totally involved. As others told stories he leaned toward them, sometimes with his eyes closed, as if trying to get a sense of their lives as deeply as he possibly could.

When the talking stone was finally passed to him, this rather burly man, a twenty-six-year veteran of the force, sitting with fourteen other officers and fifteen members of the public, spoke with simple eloquence of his life, first as a human being "just like you" as he said to others in the circle and then "as an officer of justice."

His story focused on the prejudice he felt against him because he was a police officer.

"People see me and automatically think I'm out to get them, no matter what," he said, "even when I'm there to help. And I can tell you that if I arrest someone with dark skin, more often than not he thinks I'm singling him out because of the colour of his skin—that I'm a racist. It doesn't make sense. I get up in the morning just like everyone else. I hug my three girls goodbye, never knowing whether I'll come home that night. I try to do a good job, to be a good cop."

Tears appeared in the corners of his eyes. Others in the circle, sensing the world from within his eyes, would never feel the same about "cops" again.

During the same circle, a woman who had immigrated to Canada recently from Central America told a story I will never forget. Her country was involved in a civil war, which, as she put it, "never seemed to end." One morning as she and other members of her family were getting ready for the day, several guerrilla soldiers with automatic weapons burst through the door and, screaming something about her father being a government agent, began firing indiscriminately. Her mother pushed her to the floor and lay on top of her "to take the machine gun bullets." She survived there as her mother, brothers, sister, and father were shot to death.

I don't know if any of those in the circle experienced true deep empathy with her given the depth of pain implied in the story; probably not. But I can guarantee you that whatever they experienced, they would never see her as a category again.

9

altruistic love

Altruistic love is a total gift of self,
a total support of the other's welfare,
a wish for the full flourishing of the other
in his individuality for his sake.
—Mary Rousseau

Rousseau continues, "I love you for all of who you are, who you have been, who you will be, who you might have been, are not, and never will be."

Altruism is an exceptionally powerful quality of character in living community. We see it, for example, in Mahatma Gandhi's profoundly simple suggestion that we base our desire for material acquisitions on needs rather than wants, e.g.:

I want an expensive house.	*I need shelter.*
I want a fur coat.	*I need warmth in winter.*
I want fame.	*I need an opportunity to develop, nurture, and express my gifts, talents, and abilities.*

As an altruistic person I wish you well and will support you when I can as you fulfil your needs and achieve self-actualization.

This seems easy enough, but how often do we actually feel altruism within and express it with others? Or do we only say we do?

Suppose I am a father or mother with my new-born child in my arms standing in the surf with the ocean behind me. My partner stands on the beach some distance away. As a result of some disturbance on the ocean floor, a large wave forms and rolls toward me. When I turn and see it coming, I realize, in a split second, that I have enough energy and time to do one of two things. I can throw my baby to my partner and save her life. As I do so, the wave will consume me and I will lose my own life. Or I can throw my baby over my head into the wave, run to my partner, turn, and watch my baby being consumed by the wave.

What is my first impulse with my baby? I can imagine circumstances in which my choice might be complicated, but in this scenario I would probably give up my life to save my baby's life. I feel and will express altruism with my baby. And I probably feel this kind of deep altruism with my older children, perhaps even with my partner, my parents, my siblings, and others with whom I am very close.

But do I feel it with my neighbours or friends? Or, even more extremely, do I feel it with strangers? Could I stand before a stranger and say the following? "With everything I am, with everything I have, with everything I do, I wish you your hopes and dreams. I don't know you at all, but, assuming you will act within the law and moral principles of the society in which we live and are a reasonable and caring person, if the achievement of your hopes and dreams depends on my life, I will give my life." To what degree, at what depth, do I wish others well—and mean it?

These are not realistic scenarios, of course. They are in some ways silly examples because they would never happen. But the point is clear. Altruism in living community is a fundamental quality of character that implies we care for each other deeply, all of us, and are ready to support each other whenever we can.

What if a couple engaged in a serious argument began with altruism? What if two teenagers in conflict began with altruism? What if those facing important negotiations in business assumed altruism? What if we all assumed altruism with everyone? Utopia—an ideal world that could not possibly exist!

the individual in society

The world was not left us by our parents;
it was lent us by our children.
—African proverb

The expression of talents and abilities is vital in community. It is important for each of us to support and respect the talents and abilities we find in others.

I won't forget the time my daughter came home from school when she was seven or eight, in second grade, I think. She was glowing with pride. "Guess what, Daddy?" she said. "My friend Catherine passed another level in mathematics.

She's already doing problems in the third grade book."

I remember another experience. My daughter came home late from school one day. She was in the sixth grade. She looked depressed. "I just can't catch up to Catherine in math," she said in a frustrated voice. "I work on math every day. No matter what I do, she always gets a better grade."

When she was young, my daughter was happy for Catherine. She felt good about her friend's talents. Under the influence of the school and her peers she became competitive with Catherine. Her sense of esteem began to suffer. She could no longer be truly supportive. We cannot afford this human destruction.

This kind of thing can happen within a family when one sibling does not wish the best for another or when a parent or parents are threatened by the talents of a child. The biology of gender can enter this picture. A woman (or man) is rewarded for certain activities and not others with little consideration for her (his) particular talents and abilities.

And obviously, this kind of thing can happen at the level of society. I mentioned my interview with Ervin László.

He said this: "As we attempt to nurture diversity, we must remember how important our work is. The danger of the subordination of an individual is evident in the recent experience of the Holocaust. If Hitler had won the war, for example, he might have created a thousand-year Reich in which the individual was totally subordinated to the system. The same thing could have happened under Stalin. And given the techniques for controlling behaviour that we have at our disposal, it is not impossible that systems could arise in which individuals are nothing more than cogs in a machine. Perhaps we ought to optimize evolution on the level of the individual and then allow it to unfold on the level of society."

are stars really that hard to find?

If you obey all the rules, you miss all the fun.
—Katharine Hepburn

We used to read a story to our children about a man who lived in a house in a neighbourhood in which all the houses looked alike.

This man had a gift for expressing himself through colour. So he painted his house many colours and decorated it with flowers and such.

"What is he doing?" the neighbours wanted to know. "He's ruining the neighbourhood."

After a while, however, a neighbour came over and stayed for a glass of lemonade on the man's front porch. Something happened: he got caught up in the man's delight, let go of his negative judgement, and went home to paint his own house to look like the ship he had dreamed of all his life.

Of course, one by one the other neighbours painted their houses to fit their dreams. Before long the neighbourhood was the most interesting in the city.

It is tragic that, as a culture, we do not celebrate the expression of diverse talents, abilities, and intelligences. This mindset may be dangerously maladaptive in the long run.

We can tie material reward to responsibility and accomplishment. But to what degree? In my culture, for example, there are ample rewards for talent for movement in athletics. We do not reward talent for movement in dance as much. We celebrate talent for administration in business. When this same talent is applied in education, we consider it less valuable, secondary.

Of course we need to take responsibility for how we shall support ourselves, which might imply thinking ahead so as to prepare for a profession. Often this takes enormous discipline. But how much creativity and positive change might we reap—how much better might we live?—if each of us was given the opportunity to explore and express our talents and abilities with true appreciation from others including reasonable financial rewards?

mutual trust

Only with the support, insight and fellowship of community can we face the dangers of learning meaningful things.
—Fred Kofman and Peter Senge

A fifth quality of character, *mutual trust*, is fundamental for those who wish to live community. But they view trust differently than we do in today's societies. We worry about "the other guy." Will he treat me right? Will he try to take advantage of me?" The key questions relevant to a definition of trust are about others. "Can I trust you?" or, "Have you earned my trust?" or, "Have or will you do anything to violate my trust?" Unfortunately, we never know with absolute certainty whether we can trust others. After living with someone for ten or twenty years we can be reasonably sure she is worthy of trust. But the chance is always there. Tomorrow she may do something to prove us wrong.

To live community, we begin with a different question: "As I stand before you, can I trust myself never to do anything knowingly to hurt you? I may make a mistake. I may be unclear. I'm not perfect—consciously together and aware of all my psychological motivations every moment. But can I trust myself to do my best?" The question is obviously rhetorical. I carry self-trust within me in your presence.

In the rapidly changing world in which we live today, the first question—"Can I trust you?"—is almost impossible to answer. We rarely know each other long enough to earn or prove trust with each other. The answer to the second question does not depend on time. It depends on character. If I can trust myself in your presence and you can trust yourself in mine, we can experience trust together the moment we meet. When each person is capable of self-trust, trust in a gathering can happen in an instant.

Let's explore this second kind of trust with a child's game. We find an open space, thirty of us, about twenty or so feet in diameter. We imagine it is a lovely, grassy field in spring. We enter the circle. Each of us imagines we are alone in the circle, happily meandering slowly here and there as if in a dreamy reverie. A voice calls out some instructions. "As you walk, choose one other person in the field. Don't let them know you chose them, but place them in your mind. Now pause where you are and ask yourself a question: 'Can I trust myself never to do anything knowingly hurtful to the person I am thinking of?' When you are able to answer the question 'Yes,' begin to meander slowly in the circle again, here and there."

After a while the voice enters again: "Now choose a second person without letting them know you have chosen them. When you have chosen this second person, pause where you are in the circle and ask yourself the same question: 'Can I trust myself never to do anything knowingly hurtful to this person?' When you are able to answer the question 'Yes,' begin to meander slowly again."

Then the voice gives the final instruction: "Now form a perfect equilateral triangle with your two people in silence. Don't let them know you have chosen them as you do this."

And the laughter begins. Of course, there are hundreds of thousands of possible arrangements of people in triangles in such a field (circle). We go on and on moving and moving because every time one of my "partners" moves I must move, and then whoever has chosen me must move, and so on and on.

The obvious point of this kindergarten activity is that we are all connected such that whatever we do affects thousands, if not hundreds of thousands of people around us. So if we trust ourselves with others they will be affected. They will learn that self-trust in the presence of others can be magical. And it is fun.

13

from domination
to partnership

We don't need more explanations.
We need to shorten the distance
between who we are and how we act.
—Isabelle Stengers

The qualities of character probably come from three primary sources. Some may be pre-programmed genetically in all human beings. Lionel Tiger suggests a tendency to care for others, especially those close to us biologically, may be one such characteristic. As I mentioned above, some may be the result of what Ernst Mayr called "open pre-programming." We probably enter the world with the potential to feel empathy and sense similarities with others. Whether we do so may depend on beliefs and values we develop during our lives about family and friends. And other qualities, of course, are not connected to pre-programming. They depend completely on personal history and culture.

Whatever the source, the qualities of character seem important to most of us. If they are, why don't we simply nurture and express them everywhere all the time? We dream of living this way. Why not "inject reality into the dream," to borrow a phrase from Delacroix?

One of the people I spoke with as part of the project I mentioned earlier was an interesting and provocative woman named Riane Eisler. At the time of our conversation, she was developing ideas outlined later in *The Chalice and the Blade*. She suggested social, political, and economic structures and systems in most societies were and are organized in hierarchies held together by habits and principles of domination. In these "dominator societies" everyone both dominates and is dominated by others. No one gets off the hook. Illegitimate power, greed, and self-righteousness are commonplace.

Eisler compared these societies with "partnership societies" in which people do responsible activities separately and together and earn legitimate authority. Personal power is expected and guaranteed. Interpersonal power disappears. Individuals develop and express gifts, talents, and abilities in mutual respect. "You do leadership well," a person might say. "Would you please be the foreman for a while? I prefer to build furniture. I am happy to follow for a while." In partnership societies, people meet their needs to be creative as individuals without sacrificing their duties and responsibilities in the group.

Why don't we live the way we wish to with each other? Eisler's metaphor seems as appropriate as any. We are born into dominator societies. Our dreams of community, of partnership, are no match for the habits of power and control that govern so much of what we think, feel, and do.

How can we break these habits of domination? How can we journey from domination to partnership? We "inject reality into the dream" by living the qualities of character all the time.

14

a journey "in community"

Out beyond ideas of wrongdoing and rightdoing
there is a field. I will meet you there.
—Rumi

I mentioned my talking stone earlier. I have carried it with me for many years. It was given to me by a woman from the Carrier Nation in north-central British Columbia. She explained she had found the stone during a powwow the summer before.

It was lying in a mountain stream sparkling in the sun. She thought it must be unique, one of a kind. In her words, "There couldn't be another stone like it anywhere in the universe, and for that reason alone it is precious." And of course each one of us is unique and distinct and, for that reason alone, precious.

Then, when she picked up the stone to hold for a while, she noticed it had an interesting, almost delicate structure. "It has six layers," she said, "each smaller than the one beneath it." It seemed to be shaped by unknown hands to symbolize circles of waves, ripples spreading from similar stones dropped into still waters.

"The stone is unique and separate now," she said. "But at some point during its lifetime it was part of a larger stone. And that stone had been part of a mountain. And the mountain part of the earth and the earth part of the universe." And then she said, and I will not forget her exact words as we stood outside the longhouse overlooking Williams Lake, "This little stone is part of everything, everyone, and all." The stone will always be part of everything, everyone, and all for me. And, of course, you and I will always be part of everything, everyone, and all.

I hiked to the top of an absolutely extraordinary mountain called Moon Rock near the Fraser River in the interior of British Columbia the other day. The view was breathtaking. The river had cut into sandy loam soil and left mounds, steep mounds, of sand rising to pasture lands dotted with ranches. Because of the play of the sun—the sun was high, just before noon—the deep green grass actually looked purple. A small range of mountains rose on the other side of the pastures.

The flash of sound over my head turned out to be two bald eagles rising in the updrafts created by the cooler water of the river in the hot sun. There seemed to be hundreds of birds. I don't know the names of birds. I only know the wonder as they fly nearby. The woods below me were filled with insects, mosquitoes and black flies mostly. But the breeze on my rock, for the moment at least, kept them away.

What an ocean of nature, a magnificent ocean of nature we are all part of in living community!

part two:
creative communication

15

how it was and yet might be

Kurt Vonnegut said he was more frightened of the past than of the future. The past has certainly turned out to be a worthy adversary. Perhaps we can come together to change the future.
—Kenneth Boulding

In the early 1940s, Shannon and Weaver developed the sender-receiver model to explain communication via telephone lines. It went like this: I formulate a message and send it to you. You receive it and formulate a response. In *The Seven Habits of Highly Effective People*, Steven Covey suggests that between the sender and receiver there is a space where interpretation takes place.

These models make sense in the objectified world of the dominator society. I act, you react, you act, I react, in an unending cycle, like automatic machines. Or, for Covey, I act, you interpret, you act, I interpret, I act . . . This gives us a certain feeling of security, I suppose, in that as we speak and respond we gradually get to know what the facts are.

We can turn to any newscast to find this world.

"The fact of the matter is," one commentator says, "if we do this, our health-care system will fail."

"The fact of the matter is," says another, "if we don't do this, our health-care system will fail."

Then the two speakers argue about which fact is right and true. Maybe they come to an agreement, maybe not.

Here's another example. Suppose I say, "This is my son. That's a fact," referring to my biological offspring or my adopted boy. And you are from a culture in which the person you call "son" is the child of your sister and her husband. And you say, "This is in fact my son." I, of course, call your son nephew. And I want to say, "Will the real son please stand up?" What to do? It's not easy to grasp the point that "son" is a meaning we use for the person we call "son" rather than a fact. But it is.

And to choose a very tough example, I say, "Abortion is a sin." You say, "The choice to have an abortion is my right as a woman." The lines are drawn—extreme lines that at times lead to the murder of doctors who perform abortions. We both are wrong, of course, to act as if our beliefs here are facts. They are meanings. And we have room to talk about meanings with sanity guiding our deliberations.

Actually, if you have a different opinion from me I want to learn as much as I can from you. Tell me more about what you believe. I want to learn everything with you. What is the meaning of abortion to you? Why do you have that belief? Who do you talk with about abortion? What do they believe? What do your parents think about abortion? What writers do you turn to learn about abortion? What have you learned from them? We'll talk later, when I discuss making decisions, about such deep interest in the meanings of "the other" when people have differences.

I have suggested human qualities such as genuine interest, acknowledgement, deep empathy, altruism, and mutual trust can help us find a world of creative partnership and mutual caring in living community. The problem with the sender-receiver model is it throws us, willy-nilly, back into an objectified world where partnership and caring are not easy to achieve. What model of communication, then, can support and enhance this other world so many people wish to live in?

the pebble game:
a metaphor

*Metaphors are gifts of meaning. Without them
we would indeed live in a barren world.*
—George Lakoff

As human beings we are constantly creating
meaning from experience as we communicate. In
the sender-receiver model, that meaning is often
programmed—based on opinions or beliefs we
"know to be true." What if we changed our orien-
tation in communication? What if we focused on
meaning from "experiential reality"* in a partner-

---

*I first heard this term in my interview with George Lakoff as part
of the project I mentioned earlier. It has important implications for
communication in living community.

ship world rather than on assumptions and facts? Meaning comes from experience and reality, after all, so why not find ways to join them in creative communication?

In only the time it takes to breathe I can listen to your words, your meanings, and then share my words, as meanings, with you. The experientially real words can come from the past, the present, or in anticipation of the future. Put another way, we can speak with each other rather than to each other.

This approach is difficult to explain so I have developed an experiential metaphor I call The Pebble Game to illustrate how making room for meaning can change our sense of what creative communication can be like. The Pebble Game is not about winning or losing. It has no point in the traditional sense. It is simply an exploration of a different way to think about and practice communication that enriches possibilities and potential in our interactions with others.

People often turn to metaphor when they wish to be clear with others about something they find difficult to explain or describe. "Life is a tree," I say. What I mean by this is that, for me, life has roots. It has a central core, a trunk. It has branches of exploration. Sometimes I crawl out on one or another of those branches, slip, fall to the ground, and climb up again. Life has seasons of growth and renewal and times of rest. And so on.

Or, to choose another metaphor, "Life is a journey." In this metaphor, I see life as an adventure. I travel along a path or road toward a destination. Sometimes I come to dead ends and turn back. I encounter forks and choose directions. I experience bumps in bad weather. Sometimes the way is clear.

When we choose metaphors, of course we emphasize certain meanings and not others. Life as a tree is different from life as a journey. And the meaning of The Pebble Game metaphor is dramatically different from the metaphoric meaning of competitive games.

17

playing the pebble game

Meaning comes to life when we are truly free in communication with each other.
—Elise Boulding

Before the game begins, each "player" collects one hundred or more stones of various colours, sizes, and shapes. Some people come to the game with beautifully polished stones they have bought in a store or polished themselves. Others bring stones they found in the woods, on a beach, or at the end of a country road. I used to think store-bought stones and natural stones would look odd together, but I have come to realize such diversity creates a beauty all its own.

The stones will become symbols of meaning during the game. At the beginning they are placed in piles beside each of the four or five players who gather to play the game. The "field of play" is an open circle about three feet in diameter, surrounded by an imaginary line, like children might create to play a game of marbles. The open space should be white or of a light, neutral colour so the stones stand out during the game. When I do workshops I bring white cloths with me that were cut and sewn in circles by a friend.

In any kind of communication, people follow rules, either consciously or unconsciously. Otherwise there would be chaos. Communication in The Pebble Game is no exception.

Rule One: The game is played in silence. So before they begin, players decide who will go first and which direction they will go.

Rule Two: Players take turns. On her turn, a player has three options.

Option One: She may choose any stone from the stones she has beside her. She may place that stone anywhere she wants in the circle. She may not drop or throw the stone. She must place it carefully where she wants it to be.

Once a stone has been placed in the circle, it may not be touched or moved again by anyone. It remains in its original spot for the rest of the game. Just like a word. Once a person says a word, she cannot not have said it. She can say more about it. She can apologize for having said it. But it remains in the world of meaning nonetheless. Words are precious that way.

Option Two: If she can find a way to do so, a player may balance her stone on top of another stone without moving it.

Option Three: A player may pass and save her stone(s) for a future turn, up to five turns in a row. To do so she shows her stone to the other players and then places it beside her outside the circle, separate from her other stones. When she chooses to play again, she must play all the stones she has saved to that point plus the one due on the turn. If she passes for four turns, for example, thereby saving four stones, and chooses to play on her next turn, she must play five stones, the four she has saved and the one due on her turn. She may not play two of the saved stones and save two for later. It gets too complicated when players do this.

Once a player plays her saved stones, she may return to playing one stone on each turn, or she may choose to pass and save a stone or stones again. That is, players may pass and save (up to five stones in a row) as often as they wish during a game.

And that's all there is. Sit in a circle in silence, take turns, play one stone, balance a stone on top of another stone, or pass and save stones on each turn (up to five turns in a row).

The game has no formal beginning or ending. It simply starts and stops in space and time. As I mentioned a moment ago, the game has no point, in the traditional sense. There is no winning, no losing. It simply is—an experience, a flow, an unfolding of meaning.

I am reminded of a story Bruno Bettelheim used to tell about a child he was working with in a therapy session. He introduced a game to the little boy as a part of the process. The boy asked immediately, "Is this a winning game or a fun game?" Then he said, "I don't like winning games."

The Pebble Game is a fun game.

a pebble game story

Part of the challenge in any situation in a community is to find common ground through imagination.
—Tarzie Vittachi

I remember a Pebble Game from a number of years ago. Thirty people from all walks of life were gathered for an educational program at a First Nations (native) retreat centre in Northern British Columbia. The setting itself was magnificent—a large, circular room, fifty feet or more in diameter, built in the shape and form of a teepee. Huge poles made of Douglas fir logs, almost two feet in diameter, supported the wooden walls of the teepee. They joined to form a skylight forty feet above.

The participants set up six Pebble Games, five players in each game. They played for about an hour, at which point I suggested they pause, talk about the experience, and then pick up the stones. One person spoke, as if representing everyone. "Don't you touch these stones," he said. "We're just getting started." And back they all went to their games—for another hour or so—to the end of our scheduled time together for the day. Again I suggested we end the games and move on. And again the players refused. They found the custodian and arranged to save the games untouched over night so they could return to them in the morning. The next day several of them brought cameras. They played for a while longer and then took pictures of the games for posterity.

"If you create boredom, disorder, stupidity, during your game," I often say at the beginning of a game, "take credit for it. If, on the other hand, you create pattern, beauty, excitement, wonder, take credit for that." Stones placed in a circle in silence! What could be simpler? Yet thirty players in a teepee—youth, elders, males, females, whites, natives, Sikhs, Christians, police officers, politicians, teachers—discovered and expressed something so meaningful and profound that, although they could barely find words to describe it, they preserved it until the very last possible moment.

What is it that occurs in the game? After all, there are no clear objectives, nothing to be accomplished, no predetermined outcome. Sometimes participants feel confused, lost, tentative, even frustrated. But only for a while.

Occasionally, as I mentioned earlier, I ask players to switch places in their own games. After they have played in their new positions for ten or fifteen minutes, I ask them to move to different games. When another ten or fifteen minutes have passed, I suggest they return to their original places in their original games.

Finally, I suggest they let their games come to an end and take a few minutes to walk around the room so they can see each game separately and all the games together. Without exception, when people get back together they can't wait to explore what happened—to explore the meaning of the metaphor.

"I was creating a pattern. It was frustrating when you added stones and changed it. Then after a while the new pattern became interesting."

"I noticed that I placed stones in circles. I seemed very organized. That's the way I am in my life."

"Your organization was interesting. I felt the same way. But at one point I decided to just place my stones down randomly. No matter what I did, eventually my random stones seemed to fit logically into some relationship with other stones."

"I felt like I was telling a story with my stones. When you played your stones near mine the story changed."

"It felt nice to create something together without being forced to do anything."

I have felt palpable relief in participants as they engage together with curiosity, ease, intention, and a certain kind of intimacy. Without words there is still meaningful communication. Without words there is a deep sense of community. How—carefully—do we go forward from here?

meaning and the nature of power

*We cannot afford to do again what we have done
so often in the past, replace power with power. A
kinder, gentler football will not do.
It is time to play a different game altogether.*
—William Reckmeyer

Among the many obstacles to creative communication, the seemingly infinite guises of power
can be particularly difficult to deal with. Whether
it is articulated straight up or merely insinuated in
a glance or indefinable shift of energy, we know
the face of power instinctively. And when we see
that face of power, we prepare to avoid or to
defend. Neither of these states feels good.

And so it seems particularly important to note that in The Pebble Game power disappears completely.

"Who controls what you do with the stones?" I ask each player. And each answers, "I do." Each player chooses what to do with her stones based on her experience at any given moment. She may be influenced by others. If one player places a stone on the exact spot another player had her eye on, the second player may have to choose another spot. Or one player may change her sense of what's happening in a game as others place their stones and, as a result, change what she intended to do with a stone (or stones) on her next turn. But each player remains in charge of her stones.

In other words, each player has personal power, born not as an objective of the game but as a natural outcome of the process of the game itself.

Personal power, in turn, begets feelings of self-confidence, self-respect, and self-esteem. Players say that because they feel good about themselves, it is easy for them to feel good about others.

From this basic experience, players learn they need not take offence from any stone that is placed in the circle, since no meaning can be perceived as "about" them personally. My stone is about me. I can place my stone on top of your stone and say, in my mind, "Stop putting your stone where I want to put mine." But I cannot control your behaviour. Gradually I learn it is still up to me to decide how I feel. You, in turn, control your "response." You may feel frustrated; you may be amused. There you are, creating your meaning in the game.

And so, as the game continues, meaning and experience deepen. I am together with you and I am alone, in the game. That is, I'm in charge of what I do. Each of us is separate and free, whole and complete in ourselves. Because we are free, we can make meaning with others as they, in turn, make meaning with us. We are alone together. That is why mutual meaning without interpersonal power can happen. We are always on an explore of meaning together.

This is the beginning of creative communication uncontaminated by innuendos of power.

To highlight the insanity of power plays in communication I sometimes try a little experiment in workshops. I ask for someone to play my teenage son or daughter. We agree to play a modified Pebble Game with the rules of domination and control in force. The argument is about the fact the child has stayed out late for the third night in a row and the father is angry about it. As we speak we throw our stones at each other. Most games go something like this.

Where the hell have you been, Nicholas? I told you to be home by eleven. It's past midnight.

Out with my friends.

That's not good enough, young man. Your curfew is eleven, period.

I'm old enough to take care of myself. None of my friends have to be home at eleven.

I don't care about your friends. As long as you live in this house you'll abide by the rules.

OK, I'll move out.

Then, to highlight the joy of creative communication in living community, we play The Pebble Game, following the simple rules of that game. As we speak, we place our stones into the circle carefully. Everything changes.

Where have you been, Nick? I've been worried to death.

I was with Nancy and Jack out at The Flats. There was no telephone so I couldn't call. Jack didn't want to drive home until late.

But this is the third time you've come home late this week. I thought we agreed the curfew would be eleven. What's up?

We did. But that was last year, Dad. I think I should be able to stay out later now.

We can talk about that if you want. But let's decide on a new time together, OK? Until we do, you need to stick by our agreement.

Power-hungry dominators disappear and become caring partners. The Pebble Game is easy. Differences in legitimate authority still exist, but the process is creative rather than destructive.

meaning and personal responsibility

It is difficult to hurt another with whom you feel connected as a human being in human nature.
—West Churchman

"This focus on meaning and personal power is easier said than done in the 'real' world," a person might say. "I have no control over my reactions sometimes. They are visceral. They happen automatically in my body. And sometimes I have feelings that simply come up when someone says or does something. I don't know where they come from."

This is right, particularly with reactions triggered by things like fight-flight mechanisms in the human brain. When a loud noise shatters her reverie, a person doesn't settle quietly for a moment to experience and create meaning. She is startled. She turns to the noise or jumps from her chair, unable to control her reaction. Fight-flight mechanisms are deeply embedded in human beings, probably guided by instinct and useful for survival. They are not subject to the kind of conscious perspective implied in The Pebble Game.

Some of the thoughts and feelings that "simply come up" when someone says or does something, may be based in biology. But more often than not they are connected unconsciously to experiences and meanings from the past. You call me an idiot. I react with anger, unaware your words re-stimulate my sense of inadequacy, which, in turn, is connected to my life as a child with a domineering father.

You say, "Joe, you're an idiot" (stimulus). I say, "Who do you think you're talking to?" (response). You are powerful—in complete control. You "got me." I might just as well say, "Who do you think you are, Dad?" He's the real object of my reaction. I'm stuck in a dead, unconscious memory.

But suppose you say the same thing, and I take a moment to experience and create meaning consciously from living memory and say, in a relaxed manner, "Gee, I guess you don't know me very well." You might say under your breath, "Yeah, he's still an idiot," but I gave you an opportunity to have a different experience, to create a different meaning, to live community.

I was walking with a friend in a large department store recently. She had participated in several workshops with me and completed a ten-day intensive program on community and communication. She had been born in Africa of Indian parents. She was a Hindu by faith.

As we entered one of the shopping aisles we heard the voice of a man in the next aisle. "Those Pakis ought to go back where they came from," he said angrily.

I nudged my friend, "Do you want to or shall I?" I asked.

"Go ahead," she said.

I knew I was safe from physical harm in a very public place. So I walked around the corner of the displays to the next aisle and approached the man, who was wearing a sheepskin jacket and a cowboy hat. I said, in a quiet, respectful voice: "Sir, I don't know if you wanted to hurt my friend or me with your remark. You know, she's actually from Africa, let alone India or Pakistan. I doubt she was hurt because she hears that kind of remark frequently. But I still feel hurt when I am with her and people say things like that. I'm not sure why. Have a nice day."

I wasn't condescending or unkind. I have no right to be. After all, I'm certainly not perfect. I'm still caught in many of my own unconscious patterns and stereotypes. As I walked away he might have muttered to himself, "Indian lover." But again, I gave him an opportunity to have a different experience, to change.

Sometimes I think the focus of the work I need to do within can be caught in one, simple phrase. In dominator societies I shake hands with racists and say, "Hello, who do you think you are?" I'm self-righteous and judgemental. In partnership societies I say, "Hello, who do I think I am?" I have no right to "call you down" until I achieve perfection. And when I achieve perfection, of course I will have no need to call you down. I have a right to hold you accountable for your racist beliefs and actions. And I do so. But that does not get me off the hook for my "isms."

A critical point here: If Piaget is correct in his suggestion that human beings go through predictable, sequential stages of cognitive development, young children do not have the ability to be consciously aware of experiences and meanings in certain situations. When a father calls a child an idiot, the child does not have the maturity to feel, think, and say, "Gee, Dad, I guess you don't know me very well." As I mentioned, the message becomes a defining fact he carries with him into adulthood. Then, when he is an adult and someone calls him an idiot, he hears the "fact" and reacts. He cannot listen to the word "idiot," knowing it is only a meaning in the moment.

In other words, a certain baseline of maturity and psychological health is fundamental to the practice of creative communication. From this foundation, most individuals can become consciously aware of thoughts and feelings triggered by past experiences. They can take the time necessary to control and then reshape those thoughts and feelings as they experience and create meaning in the present time.

first, do no harm—but cover your back

With perspective we can change our considera-
tion, our imagination, our anticipation of reality
and, in turn, change what we do in the world.
—Ruth Nanda Anshen

Personal power must be handled with care. It may take time for someone who has never experienced confidence in speaking honestly to find a place of balance with her new-found feelings of freedom and entitlement.

I use the phrase "personal power with responsibility" to emphasize that, just because we assume an absence of interpersonal power in communication, we do not have licence to speak without caring and regard for others. Chances are most people with whom we interact day-to-day have not considered the possibility that comments from others are meanings not facts.

In other words, it is totally inappropriate to shake your fist and scream at someone, rationalizing this callous behaviour by saying, "If you experience fear, it's your problem. If your fear is directly related to past abuse, it's your obligation to be clear about it." Words carry powerful meanings for all of us, no matter what level of awareness we are able to muster. It is our responsibility to temper our words with caring and perspective.

Nor should we be naïve about the "real" world, where the line between spoken and physical violence can be difficult to discern. If someone is about to assault you, it's the wrong time to open an exploration of the meaning of abuse. Rather, you must use all the skills you have to keep yourself safe. I am not, in the words of Naomi Wolf, "a power averse utopian." Sometimes I might need to fight back.

In the end I have the dominator skills I need to survive in the "real" world. At the same time,

I have skills in creative communication. In many situations, I can relax and enjoy the freedom to share mutual meaning with someone. Other times I might need to confront someone's behaviour or words in a direct way, even "pulling rank" in order to preserve safety or order.

Knowing I have a choice in itself changes the way I relate to those around me.

key implications
of the pebble
game

*Individuals who have fundamental qualities of
character and practice open communication say
they feel a sense of relief. It is as if they have discovered the best possible life.*
—John Broomfield

As the game unfolds, players begin to realize
there is no best player in the circle. Nothing automatically makes a person a better player—gender,
age, skin colour, or level of education, for example.
All players play this game equally well. They may
be different from each other as individuals with

different gifts, talents, and abilities, but they are equal as human beings. In this game, human equality is inevitable. In this game, players cannot not be equal.

I remember a wonderful game in a workshop outside of Philadelphia. The participants included board members, staff, and upper- level students from an alternative school. One of the teachers brought her eight-year-old daughter one day because her childcare had fallen through. The little girl coloured and read (and was bored) most of the time. But when we played The Pebble Game she sidled up to her mother and said, "Mommy, can I play?" And she did. And she had a wonderful time. And so did everyone in her game.

The longer the game, the more interesting, involving, even challenging, it becomes. As I mentioned before, a pattern begins to emerge as if out of nowhere, settles for a moment, and then changes into another pattern.

Later, when players talk about this, they realize there is no "it" in the game. The personal meaning one person has for a pattern at one point in the game may be different from the meanings other players have. I talked about this earlier. I may create a flower with my stones. You may think my flower is a star. And again, as I suggested earlier, you can "see" my flower when I show it to you. And I can "see" your star. And it is obvious to both of us that our patterns are not facts. They are meanings. The Pebble Game is not about facts. It is about human experience in a real world.*

Players can never predict what will happen next in The Pebble Game. So the game almost feels like a work of art. Players feel like artists not because they have great talent or have studied to become experts, but because of the way they engage with each other.

I once had the joy of sitting next to two musicians, a world-renowned pianist and a conductor, at a concert by a young pianist. During the intermission, the conductor turned to the famous pianist and asked, "How did you like his playing?" "I just loved it," was the answer, "I never knew whether that young man would fall flat on his face." That is, to paraphrase and interpret this answer, "He played at the edge of his craft and, by

*And, to emphasize the point again, this is not solipsism. Gertrude Stein got it right. "A rose is a rose is a rose." We both know that beautiful red flower is a rose. But it means different things to each of us given our life of experiences with roses. Far from making understanding impossible, this enriches understanding profoundly.

doing so, took the risk of making a mistake. I could never be sure exactly how he would play the next phrase."

That's what The Pebble Game is like. I call it "openness under ignorance of the outcome." As the game unfolds, each player's moves (each player's choices) become more and more interesting to the other players.

Recently I watched a group of people play a game for two hours with over two thousand stones. At the end of the game, they noted that, as time went on during the game, they became more and more interested in what others might do with their stones. They couldn't wait to see what would happen to the patterns in the game when others took their turns. "I knew what I wanted to do," one person said. "But I never knew what the other players wanted to do."

Questions about trust never come up during The Pebble Game. Players know they control their own stones. They know others control their own stones as well. They realize quickly that, if players could control each other, the game would soon become a rather boring representation of ideas rather than a wonderfully creative, unfolding, unpredictable process. Trust of self and trust of others seem safe and automatic in this game. I can't do anything knowingly hurtful to you, not because of a rule but because of the nature of the game.

I once had a workshop participant who was angry during a game. He slammed his stones down in the circle. He just looked silly. He soon felt silly and started laughing at himself.

Another time a player kept placing all his stones in a row in front of him. On the last play of the game the person across from him in the circle reached over the line and put a tan stone close to him. He was upset because he was building a fort. It turned out that she was putting the sun on the horizon. They both had a good laugh as well.

As I said earlier, at several points during games, players try to imagine what patterns might look like from other points of view. They try to see from within the eyes of other players—to get a sense of what patterns mean to them. Players never know, of course, whether they are right. But the sensing itself is fun. It makes the game more interesting. "Now where did that move come from?" a player thinks to herself. "What does my partner see? What does she wish to create?"

If players remain quiet for a while, if they save stones for several turns, they can shape (create) their own small patterns or have some reasonable impact on larger patterns in the circle when they finally decide to play. In this game, silence is truly golden.

the pebble game
with words

*Listen first to understand
and then to be understood.*
—Steven Covey

With the lessons of The Pebble Game as a foundation, we can change our approach to communication with words. Most of us are familiar with the model of communication developed by Shannon and Weaver outlined earlier. The Pebble Game implies a different model.

In The Pebble Game, one person senses meaning within. She places her meaning into the world in words. These words become a source of meaning for a listener. If she chooses, the listener can draw the words into her. She can add thinking and feeling and then place her words into the world. As this process unfolds, the two people experience and create meaning within as they find and create meaning with each other. Gradually, they become familiar with each other. They "understand" each other.

When the principles of The Pebble Game and the approaches to communication implied in the game become a foundation for the way we use words with each other, conversations are more interesting, provocative, creative, challenging—more fun. People wish to discover every nuance, every detail in their own life experiences and in the life experiences of others.

And with other potentially meaningful things like non-verbal sounds (paralanguage) facial expressions, movements, postures, odours, and colours of clothing, for example—anything that can be significant in communication—they can't wait to explore similarities and differences as they experience and create meaning separately and together. When they have to make decisions about something, they can be more effective and more productive. They can find creative alternatives in a world of possibilities.

making decisions:
the old way

Just because there is diversity in community,
we need not assume there is no unity.
—Ervin László

Let's explore an example of decision-making to clarify the nature of creative communication. And let's choose an issue that is difficult for many people to work through together, an important issue that raises fundamental moral questions.

Should a person have a right to choose euthanasia when she is extremely ill with a degenerative disease or when she is very old and wishes to "let go"?

When the sender-receiver model is the unconscious foundation of communication, those attempting to make decisions together often begin with arguments about who is right and for what reasons. In more sophisticated discussions based on this model, when people have been trained in conflict resolution, for example, or some other form of alternative dispute resolution such as Interest-Based Negotiation (see *Getting to Yes*), a discussion may take on a kinder, gentler flavour. Those involved in the discussion may use such skills as active listening to be clear about one another's positions or interests and, then, by having added clarity, try to find some way through any disagreements. One person might convince another of a particular point of view. Those involved in the discussion might find a compromise. Or, even better, they come to a consensus.

With the sender-receiver model as a point of departure, a discussion of euthanasia may unfold as follows between two people with different points of view.

A person has a right to determine when she wishes to die.

What about the obligation people have to respect nature?

Respect for nature doesn't mean people have to suffer until they die.

That's your opinion. It's wrong to interfere with a natural process.

What if the person would recover and live ten more years if euthanasia were not an option?

What if she would? She doesn't know whether she will ahead of time. And she should have the right to decide whether that possibility matters to her.

You're suggesting a person should have a right to act as if she's God, as if she has a right to make decisions about life and death.

Don't bring God into this. Euthanasia is about human beings ...

What's happening here? What kinds of statements are these two people making with each other?

"A person has a right to determine when she wishes to die." Sounds like an assumption or a belief stated as a fact.

"What about the obligation people have to respect nature?" A leading question based on a generalization?

"Respect of nature doesn't mean people have to suffer until they die." A rationalization? A justification? Again in the form of a conclusion.

"That's your opinion. It's wrong to interfere with a natural process. What if the person would recover and live ten more years if euthanasia were not an option?" An opinion in the form of a conclusion followed by a leading question that hides a rationalization or justification?

"You're suggesting a person should have a right to act as if she's God." A judgement based on a belief?

"Don't bring God into this. Euthanasia is about human beings." An assumption stated as a fact?

This is what people do in a world of senders and receivers. They debate positions or consider interests by speaking opinions, generalizations, conclusions, assumptions, rationalizations, justifications, values, and beliefs stated as facts, more or less clear, more or less reasoned, sometimes harsh, sometimes kind and careful.

25

making decisions: creative communication i

Diversity is a challenge and an opportunity.
It is critical to our survival as a species.
—Bela Banathy

Let's explore the same issue again, but let's use the model of creative communication. Before we do, however, let's review some of the goals and objectives implied in the model. In creative communication, individuals begin with self-respect and respect for each other as human beings. If at any point they start to feel negative about each other they suspend their discussion and return to one or another of the qualities of character. They become genuinely interested in one another; they appreciate one another's true gifts, talents, and abilities; they try to become as the other; they practice altruism and affirm self-trust. When they find each other as supportive, thoughtful, caring human beings, they return to the discussion.

They try to understand each other, even though they know total understanding is not possible. They know they have things in common, simply because they are human beings, so they can sense each other's lives. That's enough to get them started. They focus on "living meaning" (See below.) They tell their stories to each other. They describe and explain things that have happened to them in the past that affect what they think and feel today. They search for meaning in things they think, feel, intuit, and imagine in the present and as they consider the future.

As they tell their stories of meaning to each other, the reasons for their opinions, generalizations, and conclusions become clear. They find similarities and differences in experience and meaning. They realize intuitively they have no grounds for conflict. Their similarities draw them together. Their differences become a foundation for the discovery and creation of new meaning.

As they engage together through living meaning, they use skills in clear expression and deep listening. In clear expression, they wish to find and describe the meanings they experience and create within that are relevant in the exploration they are engaged in with others. In deep listening, they wish to find the meanings they experience and create within as they listen in the presence of others.

When a person listens deeply, her sole objective is to sense the life of another person. She begins in a place of no-thing-ness, of emptiness. She has no interest in determining whether, from her point of view, the person she is listening with is "right or wrong." If her voice of self-talk enters her stream of consciousness, she lets it go and returns to genuine interest. She doesn't "suspend" judgement; she lets it go completely for a while.

People tell me it is not possible to let go of judgement completely for a while. I know it's possible because I've seen it happen thousands of times in workshops. I recall an activity that proves the point.

Workshop participants choose a subject half of them support and half of them are opposed to such as spanking children. Each group forms a circle. Then I ask the groups to choose a person who will switch groups and become a full member of the opposite group in all areas of meaning, who will change her point of view completely and become the point of view she originally disagreed with.

In this activity the people chosen to change groups do not play the role of someone with another point of view. They empty themselves completely of all meaning. The others in the groups tell story after story based on living meaning. The chosen people make these stories their own as if they lived them throughout their lives. I have seen deep tears in this activity as the chosen people embrace a new way of seeing the world.

A typical story for one group might be the following: "I remember when I was rolling a ball down the driveway into the street. My mother came out to go shopping. When she passed me she said firmly, 'Billy, don't roll the ball into the street.' When she came back I was still rolling the ball into the street. Just as she passed me I jumped in front of a car to get the ball. She grabbed me forcefully and slapped me lightly on the bum. 'Now go in the house and play something else,' she said."

This story might reinforce a feeling that a pat on the bottom is OK in rare circumstances in which the child needs to be punished because of dangerous behaviour.

A quite different story for the second group might sound like this: "I remember when I was playing with Freddy in the school yard. We got into a fight over something. I can't remember what. I hit him in the face and broke his glasses. His father called my house and told my parents he wanted them to pay for new glasses. My Dad said, 'Alan, go upstairs.' I knew what to do. I had done it several times a month for years. I took down my pants and bent over my bed. He came up, took off his belt, and beat me until I was covered with welts. Sometimes he used branches from the willow tree in the yard and beat me until I bled. I still have the scars on my back to prove it."

This story might be part of the meaning: "Never punish a child by spanking them."

After a time I ask the chosen dyad to come to the centre of the entire workshop circle and to explore their differences about spanking. In many cases these two people have actually taken on the new point of view so they find it easy to become as their "partner." It usually takes about two minutes for them to find a place, a meaning, they both feel good about. Disagreement is replaced with understanding. Understanding, as if by magic, leads to a complete transformation of the issue.

In this example, an agreement "to act as if for a while" might be that it is OK to tap a child on the bum to reinforce the child`s safety. But it is never OK to spank a child.*

In this process of decision-making, disagreement disappears and becomes difference, and difference disappears and becomes a foundation for the creation of new meaning.

*This phrase highlights the assumption that the "agreement" is firm but, at the same time, might be changed sometime in the future.

26

creative communication: coming home

*I was coasting down from space. There was this
beautiful planet coming up, this once and future
planet. I felt such nostalgia for what we could be.*
—Ed Mitchell

Let's return to the question we considered earlier. Should a person have a right to choose
euthanasia? This time, instead of stating opinions,
generalizations, conclusions, and so forth, the two
individuals involved in the discussion search for,
discover, and explore meaning with each other.
They use living thinking and living feeling from

past experiences. Living thinking and living feeling are not like the repetitive, stuck "thoughts" David Bohm spoke about when I talked with him and the "felts" mentioned by William Isaacs in Dialogue: The Art of Thinking Together (citing the work of Peter Garrett). They are open and alive at every moment—to new insights, new perspectives, new learning.

One of the two says:

I remember when my father was dying. He had had eleven heart attacks. My mom had kept him alive over and over with an oxygen tank. Then, as his heart became weaker and weaker, his mind became fuzzy and confused. The doctor said his heart could hardly pump blood to his brain anymore.

Mom called me at college and said he was in the hospital this time, hardly able to talk. I flew home and went to see him in the hospital right away. He was hooked up to two machines that were keeping him alive.

He wanted me to be with him alone for a while. After everyone was gone he looked at me and started to cry. "Please, Jimmy, he whispered. Please—I want to die now."

To which the other replies:

My story is very different. My grandmother seemed ancient to me when I was little—all "craggy" and grumpy a lot of the time. But never with me. I used to climb on her lap and rock with her in Mom's old Shaker chair.

Then one day she fell and broke her hip and arm. The shock affected her heart so they took her to a hospital for the elderly.

Mom said it was time for her to die. "She is in unbelievable pain all the time. And she's so unhappy now because she can't ever come home. The doctor said it would only be a day or two more—unless there is some kind of miracle."

But somehow she came back to life and got well. And I got to sit on her lap again smelling her musty, old clothes and rubbing my head against the flannel.

After listening deeply with each other, can either of these individuals say, "I disagree with the meaning of euthanasia in your life?" As human beings, they can only sense, become familiar with, try to understand each other's stories as part of a process of coming to a place they both feel good about.

making decisions: creative communication ii

Understanding is a process more than a content.
It can lead to agreements which are assumptions
of familiarity rather than descriptions of reality.
—Carl Friedrich von Weizsäcker

If they wish, these two individuals can explore living meaning in many other ways. They can revisit haunting questions together: "I wonder whether Dad would have been different at the end if he had chosen to let death take its time?"

They can search for and explore deeper meanings through intuition and imagination: "What would the world be like if people never had to suffer severe pain when they were sick or old?"

They can find and explore connected meanings together: "What does he word 'right' mean in
our lives?"

They can turn to thoughts and feelings about
moral issues as they remember things they've read
in philosophy, theology, biology, and the social
sciences. "I remember the first time I read the idea
we should never treat a human being as a means
to an end, only as an end in herself. I don't know
why. I felt relieved."

They can search for, discover, and explore
meaning with others, with all kinds of people, who
have thoughts and feelings about euthanasia.

Unlike opinions, conclusions, and generalizations, living meaning never stands still. Sometimes, just by listening in the presence of others,
a person senses a change in the way she views the
subject of discussion. A subtle shift takes place,
out of awareness, in some intuitive world, and she
embraces a different point of view.

Sometimes, as people explore deeper meanings, they find comfort in difference. The need to
work through or resolve an issue disappears. They
don't agree to disagree. They enjoy living side by

side with different experiences and different points of view.

Sometimes, when people get to know each other as human beings, they no longer wish to convince each other they are right. The importance of opinions is replaced with the value of life.

Sometimes, when people are clear with each other, they discover the subject under discussion has nothing to do with their fundamental concerns. They move to other worlds of experience and meaning together.

Sometimes, a focus on experience and meaning takes people into questions about essence in human nature, about being and knowing. They search for clarity and understanding together.

"Show me a difficult issue and I'll show you at least a hundred and ten elegant solutions." I'm not sure where I read this. But it makes sense. When people search for, discover, and explore experience and meaning together, possibilities for creative living seem endless.

As I implied earlier, in creative communication individuals wish to find places of meaning they feel good about together. They continue until this happens, however long it takes. They never give up. They search for, discover, and

explore living meaning within and with each
other until something emerges between or among
them that feels OK, until they can come to an
agreement "to act as if for a while."

part three:
end notes

28

living meaning: reality and experience in human understanding

In true communication we find a quiet place, an empty soul, meaning without definition, a reservoir for the creation of familiarity.
—David Bohm

Let's look at "living meaning" for a moment with the word "book" using George Lakoff's thoughts about "experiential realism," a phrase I used earlier. Say I want you to understand my meaning for the word. Obviously, we share knowledge about the fact "book," the real thing in the world. And we know the difference between book, pamphlet, and magazine. Realism works fine for us.

But what of experiential meaning? To understand experiential meaning we turn to stories in living memory—stories that still have meaning in our lives. Through such stories we find unique meaning for each person. Again, this meaning can be understood by a listener because she is a human being, but it is based in the speaker's life.

So I'm the speaker and I am exploring my meaning with you as you live the qualities of character.

I remember when I was three years old and I was sitting on my mother's lap. She was holding a thing with a hard cover and pages with black marks and pictures on them. Her lap and chest felt soft and warm. Her voice was gentle and kind. She was wearing a fluffy blue sweater. The chair was rocking quietly. At the end she closed the thing and said, "Wasn't that a nice book?"

Then I went into my father's study. He was holding a big thing that looked similar to the book my mother had been holding. He had his feet up on the desk, and I could see the metal brace on his bad leg. The walls were covered with books, and the room felt a bit dingy. I said, "Daddy, Daddy, come play with me." And he said curtly, "Don't bother me. I'm reading my book."

So "book" is associated with love with my mother and rejection with my father. These associations will stay in my subconscious forever as meanings. They come from language in use. When we share meanings from the real world and meanings from language in use we can understand each other very deeply.

This is "living meaning." It comes from living memory, which includes every experience we have had with a word in the past, in the present, and in anticipation of the future.

Many years ago I was a voice coach for singers in Broadway musicals in New York City. I taught them to build living meaning for the important words in a song. For example, the word "summertime" in the song of that name from *Porgy and Bess*. First they created living meaning for the words in their lives. Then they did the same for the words as they came up in the lives of the characters they were playing.

"I remember when I was sitting with a friend on Negril Beach in Jamaica, West Indies," one of them might say. "The sun was high and hot. My friend turned to me and said, 'Summertime is unbelievably hot here,' as a bead of sweat dropped from his forehead onto his nose."

Or "I remember when I was sitting in the back yard reading *Freedom* and my sister came out with her newborn baby. The baby was gurgling and laughing in the breeze. My sister said, 'What a lovely day. I love summertime.'"

When the singer performed the song, she did not think of the experiences of living meaning she had discovered. She concentrated on the meaning of the words at that moment in the life of the character she was playing. But all the living meaning was there, out of awareness, in the song, and that made all the difference. The living meaning made the song unbelievably beautiful and powerful. The audience didn't know why, but they were enraptured.

We all know great singers who bring meaning to life in a song. They are not necessarily the ones who have the most beautiful voices. Think of Tom Waits, for example. But they are always the ones whose words are ripe with living meaning resting in experiential reality.

In our everyday lives, meanings from language in use are usually unconscious. We share the meanings of words in the real world in the present time. And that's as it should be. But living meaning is there to be mined whenever it makes sense and it is useful to do.

Three points:

This is not a reference to the idea of language in reference to socio-cultural uses. Here I refer to the uses of language by individuals in everyday life.

Agreements concerning meanings of words are partly due to structures in language that imply inter-subjective experience.

The word "understanding" itself has an interesting meaning in creative communication. I often put it this way: One goal of creative communication is to learn how to go on not understanding each other completely together forever. Of course we "understand" each other. But the perpetual process of mov-

ing and changing understanding is fundamental in living community.

sources of experience and meaning

What you are speaks so loudly over your head
I cannot hear what you say.
—Madeleine L'Engle

Each word a person speaks is filled with meaning from the past, the present, and memories of the future. And each time a person speaks a word, the meaning of that word changes somehow as it both creates and becomes part of everyday life. Words are rich with meaning. But meaning never stands still. It is always unfolding through time.

Sources for the meanings of words are many and various. They are more or less important or relevant in different circumstances and at different times. The nature of matter itself in an environment can be important in the meaning of words. Although this may seem self-evident, even mundane in contemporary social groups, it can be important in subtle, usually unconscious, experience. For example, the stone in my right hand is precious. It is completely smooth with a deep blue hue. The stone in my left hand is rough with sharp edges. If I hold it tightly it actually cuts into my flesh. Certainly the two stones have different meanings for me.

The material/physical nature of our bodies is also a fundamental source for the meanings of words. My precious stone fits nicely in the palm of my hand. I can grasp it with my opposable thumb and fingers, hold it tightly, throw it to others, catch it when they throw it back to me. It means something very different to me than does the boulder I am sitting on simply because I can grasp it in my hand. The boulder is meaningful, in turn, partly because I can sit on it. Two bits of matter, similar in internal material structure, different in my experience because of the shape in nature of my body.

Biological phenomena are important in the experience and creation of meaning among human beings. It seems clear that, although systems and structures in the brain are beneath consciousness in everyday life, they make it possible, literally, for us to sense our own lives; to engage with others in human relationships; and to think, feel, intuit, and imagine in certain ways and not others. Our brains surely limit the events we can "speak into the world."

And more of biology: I have a male body. I can't imagine sensing the same meaning for birth as my wife and partner. The meaning she experiences and creates for birth must be different from mine simply because we are different biologically. I don't mean we can't talk about birth together and find some ways to become familiar with each other, but in the deeper reaches of life, some of our meanings for the word will remain, forever, different.

My deeper biology is completely hidden from me as I experience and create meaning. I never think about whether the flow of blood in my veins affects the meaning I give to the word "run." Yet

I am certain it does. "Run" means something very different now, as my veins and arteries age, than it did thirty years ago.

Psychological phenomena in general, more or less integrated with biology, physical nature, and material things, surely influence experience and meaning in our lives. The meaning I experience when I speak the word "mother," for example, is directly related to my personality, which, in turn, is connected to the psychological world I experience and create each day. In my world, mother is a source for the meanings quiet and caring confidence with women.

My friend Matthew and I have talked about his experiences with the word "mother." Surely, because of her own psychological being related in some ways to the meanings she experienced and created for the word "mother" in her own world, Matthew's mother was, for him, an authoritarian, abusive, angry, frightening woman. In his early twenties he realized he carried a psychological life-mother with him from his experiences with his mother. He described his life-mother as a sense of hopelessness, despair, worthlessness, and a fear of intimacy with women. His psychological world, filled with experiences with his mother, led him to sense and create very different meanings for "mother" and patterns with women in his adult life than those I sensed and created.

Personal history is a rich source of meaning for human beings. Personal history includes the many things that happen during our lives, things we remember and forget and remember again, the wonderful details in daily activities that stay with us, in or out of consciousness, seemingly forever. They become more or less important to us in different moments.

My personal history does not include witnessing deaths at the hands of rival gangs. I have an African American friend in New York who has witnessed two such deaths in recent years. His meaning for "death" is certainly different from mine because the sources of that meaning in his personal history are so different from mine.

Personal history is deeply connected to another source of meaning, perhaps the primary source of meaning in our lives—human culture. Culture is an important source of meaning because it carries knowledge, values, and beliefs from so many years in the past into the present and future.

I don't mean to suggest culture is not changing. Yes, we carry knowledge, values, and beliefs from the past into the present and future. But just as does everything else, culture continues its own internal transformation. It changes ever so slightly, sometimes moment to moment, sometimes generation to generation.

Notwithstanding this change and flow, it is fair to talk about patterns of culture that last through time—distinctive patterns. The patterns are such that the culture of one group can be distinguished from that of another on many levels.

When I spend time "on reserve" with First Nations (native) people, I am struck by the meaning they give to the word "elder" and to the expression of that meaning. In my culture the word is applied to someone who is no longer important. More often than not the person lives in a facility somewhere with other elders. If she is a member of my family, I visit her once in a while. Occasionally I take my children along so they know they have a grandparent. I love her, I suppose, but I certainly don't have much to learn from her.

My First Nations friends, on the other hand, revere elders. They know they can gain wisdom if they learn to be quiet and listen when elders are present. They care deeply for elders and look after them. Elders are important in families. And they remain with those families until they die.

Clearly, the meanings I have for "elder" and those of my First Nations friends are very different as a direct result of our different patterns of culture.

As with the other sources of meaning, we often carry culture out of awareness. It remains unconscious to us as a source of meaning. The more diverse our societies become, however, the more aware we tend to be. Fortunately, our differences highlight culture.

And finally, pan-cultural experience is an important source of meaning—meaning shared by every human being. As human beings we have certain experiences in common. Some of these are from everyday life and some are what Jung called archetypes. Some are pre-programmed and some are hardwired in the brain. We are all in the world of meaning together.

act as if for a
while

Language is an expression of how we are each
moment rather than why we are forever.
—Tarzie Vittachi

"Act as if for a while." Here we go again. Isn't
that relativism? No ultimate truths. No given,
unalterable patterns. Or, in everyday life, no given
ways of thinking and feeling.

I discussed this briefly earlier. Here's an example we can grapple with that brings up the issue.

The Catholic Church has said using contraceptives is a sin. This is probably related to a
genetically pre-programmed pattern of thought,

feeling, and behaviour evident in some cultures and in some people. But is it at least possible that a hundred years from now the Catholic Church will send out an edict stating that using contraceptives is not a sin?

Every person I ask this question answers, "Yes, it is possible." So the Catholic Church has decided to act as if using contraceptives is a sin for a while.

We are learning that genes determine lots of thoughts, feelings, and behaviour. But it is important to remember that, when human experience and meaning enter the mix, the possibilities for variety in beliefs and values multiply.

This is not fundamentalism. Not any and every belief and value is available to everybody. According to recent research it actually seems some people are predisposed to have conservative beliefs and values, for example, and some liberal beliefs and values.

When a moral principle is pre-programmed biologically, lasts a long time, and is embraced by many people in many cultures, we are justified in calling it a universal truth. But responsible cultural relativism can live side by side with such reasonable, universal agreements about right and wrong. Our beliefs and values, even our moral principles, need not be rigid. But they can be clear.

It is worth noting that meta-communication is available to everybody—communication about communication. We can think about thinking and feel about feeling. This releases us from chains of rigid, unchanging opinions, justifications, rationalizations, and assumptions.

Our Diversity
is a
Foundation of Creativity

Our Common Humanity
is a
Foundation of Peace

acknowledgements

I wish to thank so many people I hardly know where to begin. Nancy Leach, my wife and partner for many years, was and is a constant inspiration. My children, Eric, Ani, and Tes Schaeffer, have kept me going with their presence in my life. Greg Cran urged me to develop a program of work on multiculturalism and brought worth to that program from the very beginning. Graham Dixon supported the application of the work in graduate leadership programs for many years. I met Paul Born in one of those programs. I learn new things every day from Paul. He is a valued friend and colleague.

I thank the workshop participants and students who, over many years, challenged me to think and feel deeply and never stop exploring and trying to understand and practice humane living. And thanks so much to the teachers, artists, novelists, philosophers, scientists, business people, and those in politics and diplomacy who granted me many hours of their incredibly busy lives in dialogues about fundamental issues facing us today.

I remember with gratitude the most important teachers in my life: Lambros Comitas, Albert Scheflen, Gregory Bateson, and Margaret Mead. Each of them had a unique vision of teaching and learning. They have influenced me profoundly in so many ways.

And my thanks to Rachel Brnjas of Tamarack Institute and Don Bastian of BPS Books for their editorial and publishing prowess in bringing this book to the light of day.

appendix a

Qualities of Character I

Living Together with Respect	COMMUNITY	*Personal Freedom with Responsibility*
"Understanding" others	GENUINE INTEREST	Self-understanding
Appreciation of others	ACKNOWLEDGEMENT	Self-confidence
Empathy	DEEP EMPATHY	Openness Honesty
Caring Support	ALTRUISM	Self-actualization
Trust of others	MUTUAL TRUST	Trust of self
	CREATIVE COMMUNICATION SENSE OF ONENESS	

appendix b

Qualities of Character II

From Dominator Societies	*THROUGH* *COMMUNITY*	To Partnership Societies
"I bet..."	GENUINE INTEREST	"I wonder..."
"I judge..."	ACKNOWLEDGEMENT	"I learn..."
"I pity..."	DEEP EMPATHY	"I sense / feel..."
"I want..."	ALTRUISM	"I / we need..."
"Can I trust you?"	MUTUAL TRUST	"Am I worthy of your trust?"
"I know..."	CREATIVE COMMUNICATION	"I mean..."
"I'm lonely..."	SENSE OF ONENESS	"I'm alone *with* you"

appendix c

The Pebble Game Metaphor

Each person is a distinct, self-creating individual.

Each individual is unique. She has a unique point of view.

No person is any better as an individual than any other person.

Many different kinds of people can take part in communication together.

Each person is in control of what she says and does. So each person is responsible for what she says and does.

No person can cause another person to interpret a given piece of information in a particular way.

No person has power over other people in communication.

Individuals make meanings together, not facts.

Conflict and difference are *in* the communication, not in the people.

Understanding, in the traditional sense of the word, is not the goal of communication. The goal is the shared creation of meaning.

Each person can try to see meaning from the points of view of other people.

All communication is open and open-ended. It is not possible to predict the outcome.

appendix d

Models of Communication

(A) THE SENDER-RECEIVER MODEL OF COMMUNICATION

GOAL:	To resolve an issue To solve a problem To answer a question
OBJECTIVE:	To understand each other
FOCUS:	Thoughts in the form of opinions, generalizations, conclusions, assumptions, rationalizations, justifications, values, and beliefs (usually stated as facts)
PROCESS:	Debate, argument, conflict resolution, the management of conflict
OUTCOME(S):	Agreements, agreements to disagree, disagreements

(B) CREATIVE COMMUNICATION: MAKING DECISIONS

GOAL: To find places of meaning we both feel good about...

OBJECTIVE: To become familiar with each other

FOCUS: Living meaning

PROCESS: Clear expression
Deep listening

OUTCOME: Agreements to "act as if" for a while

appendix e

Living Meaning

Something that happened,
is happening, or might happen

An experience ...

Something you saw, heard, read...

Thinking, feeling, intuition,
insight imagination...

Any source of meaning in your life:
from the past, in the present,
or in anticipation of the future

This meaning becomes the foundation for living opinions, generalizations, conclusions, beliefs, values, etc....

Be aware of statements that lead to dead opinions, generalizations, conclusions and values based on assumptions of fact, e.g., "The fact of the matter is..."

appendix f

Making Decisions Together

Sometimes a decision isn't necessary.

Sometimes a decision has little, if any, effect in relation to the fundamental concern.

Sometimes we can turn to finer details to become familiar with each other.

Sometimes we can choose to live among those who share similar meanings.

Sometimes we have to stay together no matter what.

Sometimes we can try an approach to the issue without coming to a decision.

Sometimes the simplest way is the best way.

Sometimes we can try arbitrary decisions for a while.

Sometimes we can live differently together.

Sometimes we find we have to suspend the decision-making process for a while.

Sometimes we can tap the meanings of many individuals.

Sometimes we have to return to the qualities of character.

Sometimes individuals with different points of view can assist each other in the creation of new meaning.

Sometimes we can ask wishful questions with each other focusing on "the crux of the matter."

Sometimes we have to return to a vision of community.

appendix g

Then and Now: Notes on Creativity

DOMINATOR SOCIETIES	PARTNERSHIP SOCIETIES
Create closed communities with "special" others	Carry community within Live in community with others
Control potential in self and others	Discover and release potential in self and others
Understand each other	Become familiar with each other
Doing *is* being I am what I do I do what I am	Being *and* doing I am and I do
Enjoy unearned authority over others (power over others)	Achieve and express legitimate authority with others (personal power)
Plan to predict and control the future	Plan "under ignorance of the outcome"
Do therapy with experts to get well	Do self-healing in the presence of others
Know facts	Explore meanings
Search for and state the truth	Search for and express meaning
State opinions, conclusions, generalizations, beliefs, and values as facts	Describe experience and meaning as foundations of opinions, conclusions, generalizations, etc.

DOMINATOR SOCIETIES	PARTNERSHIP SOCIETIES
Focus on the mind	Focus on the mind-heart-body-soul
Think and reason clearly	Think, feel, sense, intuit, and imagine clearly
Establish moral truths	Make agreements to "act as if" for a while
Compete to be the best	Co-operate in competition to achieve high levels of creativity within and with others
Play win/win, win/lose, and lose/win games	Play The Pebble Game to experience and create meaning together
Engage in interest-based negotiation to resolve disagreements	Engage in meaning-based communication to clarify differences and discover new meanings together
Begin in the middle	Begin in the beginning

about the
author

Dr. Joe Schaeffer's work offers a unique point of view about ways to build community and practical approaches in communication and the management of conflict that make it possible for us to work through difficult problems together and find joy in diversity.

Joe completed his undergraduate education at Oberlin College and New York University. He went on to Columbia University where he received an M.A. in the Teaching of English and a Ph.D. in Cultural Anthropology focusing on intercultural communication. He has taught anthropology and communication at Marlboro College in Vermont, community building and creative communication at Royal Roads University in Victoria, BC, and conflict management at Conrad Grebel University College, University of Waterloo, Ontario.

In his book *The Stone People: Living Together in a Different World*, Joe examines various models of communication we all absorb as part of everyday life. He describes the many common assumptions we have about language that keep us apart. Then he takes us on a journey to a new way of thinking about communication that makes it possible for us to live together with care and creativity.

Many people who have worked with Joe talk about fundamental changes they experience in ways of seeing things and ways of living with others. They become storytellers and witnesses as they make and share meaning. They choose to value community and partnership rather than domination and control.

The Pebble Game is Joe's signature teaching tool. It is an easy-to-learn and fun-to-play antidote to the kind of communication that emphasizes combative competition rather than peaceful collaboration. Grounded in leading theories of communication, the game positions players to feel curiosity, confidence, openness, and empathy with each other.

By embracing new and more holistic approaches to communication and conflict management, such as Joe's model of creative communication, community leaders can encourage growth and healing and promote the spirit of community.